90 days...and then

a guided journal experience

Valari Jackson

1st Edition

ISBN- 979-8-9920509-0-5

Library of Congress Control Number- pending

"The 90 days...and then Process" is pending trademark by Valari Jackson.

Welcome...

to the 90 day journal experience.

As we travel along this road together (yes, I am with you on this journey), you will unlock some powerful tools to propel you forward. Every day can be another step towards creating and sustaining the life you want to live.

Enter this space with wonder, excitement, and expectation.

If you pour yourself into this journey, you will never be the same.

When you see this symbol

Follow this qr code for deeper insight into the topic.

Is This Experience Right for You at This Time?

Because time and energy are so precious, before we go any further, let's investigate whether you are best served by going on this journey . I would hate to have you prepare for a trip that's taking you to someplace you don't want to go.

This journal draws from my own personal experience as well as feedback from my professional practice. The intention and tone of this journal are authentic, candid, and at times may be a bit difficult to digest. It is also filled with love and compassion for you. I truly want you to have a phenomenal and fulfilling life. Experience has proven that if we look at everything from a positive lens, we will not build resiliency to endure and walk through adversity. We have to call a thing a thing. We must face it head on, address why it's showing up, and assess how to remove its influence when we no longer want it around.

I have also discovered fantastic things about myself while doing this work. What a fabulous gift to be able to capture the good things and have a reasonable idea of how to repeat them and make them a regular occurrence in my life.

This journey is work. It may delve into some hidden places that you have not wanted to address; or maybe, were not aware existed. Lean into what it reveals. Trust the journey.

A Word of Caution

If at any time you are having feelings that may lead to your danger in any way, immediately seek the help of a mental health professional in your area. Call 911 immediately if you feel that you will harm yourself or someone else.

The practices in this journal are not intended to be a diagnosis or substitute for treatment that has been deemed necessary for your well-being.

Why 90 Days?

This journal was created to provide a way for you to track your progress as you move forward. The 90-day period is intended to give you enough time to design and experience a change, without pushing your accountability out so far that you feel you have plenty of time to catch up. 90 days moves quickly. By aligning your dreams and aspirations with decisive action, you increase the likelihood that you will make progress. Change takes honesty, courage, and consistency.

Your journey is separated into nine, 10-day periods. At the end of each period is the opportunity to assess your experience and progress. An honest review of how you are doing assures catching and addressing challenges early and redirecting your energy. It also allows you to highlight what is working well so that you duplicate that behavior and hit the mark to where you want to be.

How to Get the Most Impact From this Experience

Please write in this journal by hand if possible. Why? Cognitive science tells of a direct connection between the brain and the hand. Writing by hand enhances our memory and draws from the deepest part of our being.

We have been going about our lives doing what we do, how we do it. Until we are ready to face what does not serve us head on, we will get the same results that we have always gotten.

This is your nudge forward when you get stuck. Growth is not often easy, nor is it comfortable. Good news: once the blinders are off, you can't put them back on.

This is my invitation to you, to become your exceptional self. My introduction to the exceptional version of YOU.

Ready to Move On?

This journal is intended to be a confidential conversation between the two of us.

Every morning, I will ask you a few questions to uncover your intention for the day.

Every evening, we will reflect and capture how things went; and you will decide what you want more of, or less of, the next day.

Why did I create this?

Being a natural-born high achiever (a seed my parents planted), the sky has always been the limit for me. As incredible as my accomplishments have made me feel, my failures have sent me crashing into despair- at first. I have excelled greatly and then been in a position where mere breathing was almost too much for me to handle. I now see failure as feedback, and believe me... I had to do some serious work with lots of support to come to this understanding. In my opinion, which by the way is the perspective of this journal- my opinion, life takes muscle.

The muscles in our body can be weak and flimsy to start off. With regular resistance training they become stronger and more resilient. After some time our muscles build a memory of that strength and tone so that if we move away momentarily from our training, getting back into shape may not be as difficult as when we first started.

I look at the practice of journaling like building muscle. When I feel a bit off-course, it's usually because I have fallen off of my practice. Because I have built a foundation of journaling, I can usually pick it back up easily.

I created this journal as a tool for you to do the same- commit to a practice of journaling and discover all of the powerful things that happen when you do.

A Little Bit About Me

I'm a professional speaker, certified facilitator, and certified strategic intervention coach.

My professional accomplishments are anchored in more than 25 years of certifications, credentials, and commendations. I have also struggled repeatedly with moving forward and consistently being my best self. I have blurred boundaries to the point of non-existence and suffered at my own hand from exhaustion and declining health due to a misaligned understanding of my own value. I have also, with help, pulled myself from these situations with a clear resolve and commitment to take action in my purpose and move with complete confidence in my gifts and abilities. It is through this lens that I have created this experience to share with you, what has worked for me.

Born and raised in Los Angeles, CA , I am a solar-powered beach lover. I am the mother of a brilliant-in-every-way and now fully grown man, and have recently been gifted a new daughter (his wife), who lights up his life and mine. Of all the titles I have held in my life, 'friend' describes me best. True friendship, for me, spans many generations and is a relationship that grows and deepens over time. It can test our resolve and add indefinite layers of richness to our existence.

Prior to hanging out my shingle as a professional coach, I was already having what I can now classify as impactful coaching conversations with hundreds of my colleagues, family and friends. How do I know that they were impactful? Well, they told me they were, repeatedly. Because I was constantly called on to advise, direct and be a sounding board, I figured this is what happens to everyone, right?

Turns out- no. I have been entrusted with an incredible gift...and responsibility. For as long as I can remember, people have openly and easily shared their deepest feelings with me. The conversation often starts like this, " I can't believe that I'm telling you this", or " This is the first time that I'm saying this out loud" and, " I have never told anyone this before". The person speaking ranges from a trusted friend, to a stranger I meet while sitting on a bench, or standing in the coffee line, walking along the beach and even in the produce section of the grocery store. It doesn't matter.

For some reason, I seem to appear as a beacon that reads, "Tell me. It's safe here. We will figure it out together." And we usually do.

A Little Bit More About Me

It took me a while to understand what was actually happening- that these chats, under the cloak of trust and transparency, were laying the groundwork for some transformational coaching. This exercise in listening, receiving, and then repositioning before reflecting back, unbeknownst to me, was building my coaching awareness. It was while working with my own coach, Heather, that I finally started to get it. Heather and I have had many sessions that were uncomfortable for me. She drew out things that I was reluctant to say out loud and needed to hear myself say.

During one of these sessions, I shared that my now, quite successful real estate career was feeling burdensome. "I couldn't care less about the houses." I told her. "I'm sick of this business." (One of my recent transactions caused me to question my client's integrity.) An integrity mismatch will quickly disengage me from a relationship every time- whether it be professional or personal.

"What I care about", I continued, "is leading people to trust their judgment to make a reliable decision. Being a vehicle for empowerment sets my soul on fire!" And there it was. I didn't even catch it at first. Heather did. She responded, as usual, with a profound yet simple comment in a tone that resonated to my core, "That's because you're made for that." "Made for what?" I asked, becoming a bit annoyed at this point. She seemed to not even pick up on the fact that I was in a professional (and therefore personal) crisis! An entire discussion ensued, concluding with me asking the question, "Do you think I am intended to be a coach?" And then another profound response from Heather, "Uh, yeah! I'm putting down the phone for a sec to do my happy dance." Heather always had such a gift for getting right to the point while helping me see things so clearly.

A Little Bit More About Me

I consider it an incredible honor to be trusted with a person's deepest, and often uncomfortable-to-admit-to, feelings and beliefs. And as I said earlier, it is a great responsibility. As these conversations have continued over the years, I have identified some clear patterns in what keeps us stuck as well as what propels us forward.

With more than 12,000 hours on my coaching odometer, I have found one common denominator to both accounts: **mindset**.

One more important thing about me-
Although this journal is not particularly categorized as faith-based, I can't possibly convey who I am without sharing that my faith has been the foundation of my being. It is through it and because of it that I exist today.

This Journey Takes Commitment

There are a few things I will ask of you, in order for me to sign on as your traveling partner and guide.

Our Agreement:

Start today

Whichever day you hold this journal in your hand is the day you start. If it is evening, start now. Thursday in the middle of a business trip , start now. Don't wait until the first of the month, or Monday, or when you finish the invoicing or complete the project. Capture what is happening right now, because you are in the live performance of your life **right now**. The best way to move forward is to have a clear view of where you are starting from. Each day tells a story- your story, like it or not. You cannot improve what you do not measure. Track your progress. **Start Now**.

Be completely honest with yourself

Knowing where you are starting from is imperative to moving forward. Your path is different from anyone else's; your experiences in life may have prepared you differently from how someone else will approach what seems to be the same journey. You are writing this story from your perspective. Your truth, your awareness. Trusting yourself to dig in deep and pull out and examine what beliefs and practices you have held onto will allow you to decide what gets to stay. As you evolve in perspective, you will want to assure that what is inside is in alignment with what you are building.

Come back every day, no matter what
Some days you just don't feel like feeling.
Understood. Capture that. It can be as brief as you
want it to be; just don't leave the day blank.
Remember you are writing a story and the more intel
you have on the main character, the richer and more
impactful this story, and the results gained, will be.

Do something new every day
Newness brings the energy of movement, it gives
permission for change and fresh perspective.
When we make it a habit of looking for the unfamiliar,
we start to see new opportunities in our daily
circumstances. We may then welcome a new
perspective to resolving conflicts or challenges that
arise. This perspective also opens up our creativity
and zest for living.

It can be something big like visiting a new place or
something small like trying a new creamer in your
coffee. Take a different street, listen to a new
podcast, try a new ice cream flavor. The goal is to
expose yourself to getting out of your comfort zone.
Remember, there is no need for a grand gesture, just
new. You may not like or enjoy everything you try. The
new road may get you stuck in traffic and the new
podcast may turn out to be contrary to your belief
system. This is a win! Move on to the next new thing.
Even the simplest of new experiences will create new
learning pathways in the brain. Those new pathways
will offer the opportunity for new perspectives and a
new perspective can and will result in growth.

NO filters, NO editing

Even though this is a conversation between the two of us, you are the only one who will see it. Spelling, grammar, and punctuation - and dare I say it, profanity - do not matter. Get into the habit of capturing the feelings rather than focusing on the format. There may be times when a drawing will better express what you want to convey. Draw! Whatever it takes for you to be completely honest, do that. Make no apologies for expressing what has come up for you. This is about your life, and life can be messy.

Lean Into Being Uncomfortable

Growth does not happen in your comfort zone. For me, discomfort in a situation has always been the opportunity for growth and/or confirmation of misalignment with my vision and purpose. Investigate the uncomfortable feeling and quietly assess what it is telling you.

I agree
_____

Dreamcasting   Our journey together begins here

Dreamcasting is the art of bringing to the present time, a vision of what you want your life to look like at a certain point in the future.

My first experience with dreamcasting was while attending a conference. This was a gathering of nearly 6,000 people who were being coached by an international coaching company, and I was one of them. We came from all over the world to spend 3 days together focused on exponential growth in all areas of our lives. We met some of the most inspirational presenters and listened in awe as they shared their stories of how they faced challenges and overcame adversities.

The entire conference was always a phenomenal experience and the most impactful for me by far, was the dreamcasting. It was a part of the experience every year. During this time the packed auditorium that was previously filled with laughter, applause and music fell completely silent. All you heard was the sound of writing and the occasional sniffle when someone wiped away tears, as they poured themselves into consciously calling out what they wanted to see in their lives. The auditorium was filled with hope and expectancy.

This one exercise has been my go-to when I feel overwhelmed or scared, or when I lose focus on what I am doing or even why I am doing it. I am excited to now share this powerful practice with you!

A few important guidelines before we dive in:

- Find a quiet, comfortable space where you will not be easily distracted or interrupted.
- Clear your mind of any lingering thoughts or responsibilities for the moment.
- You are creating a vision for the future and capturing it as if it is happening now. Therefore you must use present tense in your writing (I am, I feel, I see...)
- Dream casting works for any period of time in the future. We are using 90 days to correspond with this journey.
- Use all of your senses as you create your day. Describe what you feel, hear, and smell around you.
- Playing baroque style classical music is helpful to this process because it relaxes the logical/analytical side of the brain and allows the creative side of the brain to flow.
- This is your story and your life. Since you can tell the story any way you want to, why not make it exciting and full of possibilities? Don't get stuck on how you will do it.

Simply **Dream** and **Cast** it out.

Grab a pen and a timer. Now write the date and time (90 days from today, at this time in the day) at the top of the next page.

Set a timer for 10 minutes. Too long? Set it for 5 minutes.

Take a deep cleansing breath. (Inhale for 4 seconds, hold for 4 seconds, exhale for 4 seconds, hold for 4 seconds.)

Now imagine yourself 90 days from now. Describe your surroundings. What will your life look like? What will be different/better? Who will be with you?

Close your eyes if that will help you see it more clearly.

Ready? Start your timer. Begin writing.

My Dreamcast   Date: Time:

My Dreamcast Date: Time:

In the Next 90 Days, I will...

Date: _____

- ○ _____
- ○ _____
- ○ _____
- ○ _____
- ○ _____
- ○ _____
- ○ _____
- ○ _____
- ○ _____
- ○ _____

90 Days

Day 1
Morning

Date: _____ Time: _____

How do you feel right now?

....
....
....

What is driving this feeling?

....
....
....

What are your guiding principles and values?

....
....
....

How would you describe your energy level right now?

Where is this energy best directed?

....
....
....

If you knew that you would succeed at any thing you tried today, what would you do?

....
....
....

Day 1
Evening

Date: _____ Time: _____

What did you do today that was new?

_____

_____

What deserves to be celebrated or acknowledged?
How did this happen?

_____

_____

_____

_____

Where did you get off track?

_____

_____

_____

How did you expose yourself to excellence today?

_____

_____

_____

Anything else on your mind?

_____

_____

_____

Complete this statement. Tonight I will rest peacefully
knowing that...

_____

_____

_____

Day 2
Morning

Date: Time:

How do you feel right now?

....
....

What is driving this feeling?

....
....
....

How do you demonstrate your guiding principles
and values daily?

....
....
....

How would you describe your energy level right now?

Where is this energy best directed?

....
....
....

If you knew that you would succeed at any thing you
tried today, what would you do?

....
....
....

Day 2
Evening

Date: _____   Time: _____

What did you do today that was new?
....
....

What deserves to be celebrated or acknowledged?
How did this happen?
....
....
....
....

Where did you get off track?
....
....
....

How did you expose yourself to excellence today?
....
....
....

Anything else on your mind?
....
....
....

Complete this statement. Tonight I will rest peacefully
knowing that...
....
....
....

Day 3
Morning

Date: _____   Time: _____

How do you feel right now?

_____
_____

What is driving this feeling?

_____
_____
_____

What do you hope for?

_____
_____
_____

How would you describe your energy level right now?

Where is this energy best directed?

_____
_____

If you knew that you would succeed at any thing you tried today, what would you do?

_____
_____
_____

Day 3
Evening

Date: _____   Time: _____

What did you do today that was new?

_____
_____

What did this new experience reveal about you?

_____
_____
_____

Where did you get off track?

_____
_____

What deserves to be celebrated or acknowledged?
How did this happen?

_____
_____
_____
_____
_____

Anything else on your mind?

_____
_____
_____

Complete this statement. Tonight I will rest peacefully
knowing that...

_____
_____
_____

Day 4
Morning

Date: _____   Time: _____

How do you feel right now?

....
....
....

What is driving this feeling?

....
....
....
....

How do you want people to experience you today?

....
....
....
....

How would you describe your energy level right now?

Where is this energy best directed?

....
....
....

If you knew that you would succeed at any thing you tried today, what would you do?

....
....
....

Day 4
Evening

Date: _____   Time: _____

What did you do today that was new?

_____
_____

What did this new experience reveal about you?

_____
_____
_____

Where did you get off track?

_____
_____

What deserves to be celebrated or acknowledged?
How did this happen?

_____
_____
_____
_____

Anything else on your mind?

_____
_____
_____

Complete this statement. Tonight I will rest peacefully
knowing that...

_____
_____
_____

Day 5
Morning

Date: _____   Time: _____

How do you feel right now?

_____
_____

What is driving this feeling?

_____
_____
_____

What do you want MORE of in your life?

_____
_____
_____

How would you describe your energy level right now?

Where is this energy best directed?

_____
_____

If you knew that you would succeed at any thing you tried today, what would you do?

_____
_____

Day 5
Evening

Date: .... Time: ....

What did you do today that was new?

....
....
....

What deserves to be celebrated or acknowledged?
How did this happen?

....
....
....
....

Where did you get off track?

....
....
....

Describe what you want to move towards.

....
....
....

Anything else on your mind?

....
....
....

Complete this statement. Tonight I will rest peacefully
knowing that...

....
....
....

Day 6
Morning

Date: .... Time: ....

How do you feel right now?

....
....
....

What is driving this feeling?

....
....
....
....

What do you want LESS of in your life?

....
....
....
....

How would you describe your energy level right now?

Where is this energy best directed?

....
....
....

If you knew that you would succeed at any thing you tried today, what would you do?

....
....
....

Day 6
Evening

Date: Time:

What did you do today that was new?

....
....

What deserves to be celebrated or acknowledged?
How did this happen?

....
....
....
....

Where did you get off track?

....
....
....

Describe what you want to move away from.

....
....
....

Anything else on your mind?

....
....
....

Complete this statement. Tonight I will rest peacefully
knowing that...

....
....
....

Day 7
Morning

Date: .... Time: ....

How do you feel right now?

....
....
....

What is driving this feeling?

....
....
....

Describe the roles you play in your life. (think of anyone who is counting on you for something)

....
....
....

How would you describe your energy level right now?

Where is this energy best directed?

....
....
....

If you knew that you would succeed at any thing you tried today, what would you do?

....
....
....

Day 7
Evening

Date: _____ Time: _____

What did you do today that was new?

....

....

What deserves to be celebrated or acknowledged?
How did this happen?

....

....

....

....

Where did you get off track?

....

....

....

Describe your feelings about the roles you play.

....

....

....

Anything else on your mind?

....

....

....

Complete this statement. Tonight I will rest peacefully
knowing that...

....

....

....

Day 8
Morning

Date: _____   Time: _____

How do you feel right now?

....
....

What is driving this feeling?

....
....
....

How do your life's roles influence how you spend your time?

....
....
....

How would you describe your energy level right now?

How would you describe your energy level right now?

Where is this energy best directed?

....
....

If you knew that you would succeed at any thing you tried today, what would you do?

....
....
....

Day 8
Evening

Date: _____   Time: _____

What did you do today that was new?

....

....

What deserves to be celebrated or acknowledged?
How did this happen?

....

....

....

....

Where did you get off track?

....

....

How does your daily routine align with what you want?

....

....

....

Anything else on your mind?

....

....

....

Complete this statement. Tonight I will rest peacefully
knowing that...

....

....

....

Day 9
Morning

Date: _____   Time: _____

How do you feel right now?

_____
_____
_____

What is driving this feeling?

_____
_____
_____
_____

What brings you joy?

_____
_____
_____
_____

How would you describe your energy level right now?

Where is this energy best directed?

_____
_____
_____

If you knew that you would succeed at any thing you tried today, what would you do?

_____
_____
_____

Day 9
Evening

Date: _____   Time: _____

What did you do today that was new?

....

....

What deserves to be celebrated or acknowledged?
How did this happen?

....

....

....

....

Where did you get off track?

....

....

....

How did you infuse joy into your day?

....

....

....

Anything else on your mind?

....

....

....

Complete this statement. Tonight I will rest peacefully
knowing that...

....

....

....

Day 10
Morning

Date: _____   Time: _____

How do you feel right now?

_____
_____
_____

What is driving this feeling?

_____
_____
_____

What do you have a non-negotiable commitment to? Who benefits from this?

_____
_____
_____

How would you describe your energy level right now?

Where is this energy best directed?

_____
_____

If you knew that you would succeed at any thing you tried today, what would you do?

_____
_____
_____

Day 10
Evening

Date: _____   Time: _____

What did you do today that was new?

....

....

What deserves to be celebrated or acknowledged?
How did this happen?

....

....

....

....

Where did you get off track?

....

....

....

What are you tired of hearing yourself say?

....

....

....

Anything else on your mind?

....

....

....

Complete this statement. Tonight I will rest peacefully
knowing that...

....

....

....

Day 10 Review

A look back as you move forward Date: _____ Time: _____

What stands out for you?

_____
_____
_____
_____
_____

What did you make progress on? How did you do it?

_____
_____
_____
_____
_____

What did you not make progress on? What happened?

_____
_____
_____
_____
_____

What surprises you most about these first 10 days?

_____
_____
_____
_____

Reflections and Celebrations

Date: Time:

Day 11
Morning

Date: _____ Time: _____

How do you feel right now?

....
....

What is driving this feeling?

....
....
....

Look back at page 22. What do you want to focus on first?

....
....
....

How would you describe your energy level right now?

Where is this energy best directed?

....
....

If you knew that you would succeed at any thing you tried today, what would you do?

....
....
....

Day 11
Evening

Date: _____   Time: _____

What did you do today that was new?

....

....

What deserves to be celebrated or acknowledged?
How did this happen?

....

....

....

....

In what areas of focus do you need support?

....

....

....

Where will you find this support?

....

....

....

Anything else on your mind?

....

....

....

Complete this statement. Tonight I will rest peacefully
knowing that...

....

....

....

Day 12
Morning

How do you feel right now?

....
....
....

What is driving this feeling?

....
....
....

How will you get going with your intentions if you must do so on your own?

....
....
....
....

How would you describe your energy level right now?

Where is this energy best directed?

....
....
....

If you knew that you would succeed at any thing you tried today, what would you do?

....
....
....

Day 12
Evening

Date: _____ Time: _____

What did you do today that was new?

....
....

What deserves to be celebrated or acknowledged?
How did this happen?

....
....
....
....

Where did you get off track?

....
....

Who have you shared your intentions with? Why ?

....
....

Anything else on your mind?

....
....

Complete this statement. Tonight I will rest peacefully
knowing that...

....
....

Day 13
Morning

Date: _____   Time: _____

How do you feel right now?

_____

_____

What is driving this feeling?

_____

_____

_____

Let's talk more about what you are creating in your life. For how long have you wanted this?

_____

_____

_____

How would you describe your energy level right now?

Where is this energy best directed?

_____

_____

If you knew that you would succeed at any thing you tried today, what would you do?

_____

_____

_____

Day 13
Evening

Date: _____   Time: _____

What did you do today that was new?

....
....

What deserves to be celebrated or acknowledged?
How did this happen?

....
....
....
....

Where did you get off track?

....
....

Why is NOW the right time to pursue your vision?

....
....
....

Anything else on your mind?

....
....

Complete this statement. Tonight I will rest peacefully
knowing that...

....
....
....

Day 14
Morning

Date: _____   Time: _____

How do you feel right now?
_____
_____
_____

What is driving this feeling?
_____
_____
_____
_____

Remember your non-negotiable commitment from Day 10? If you applied that same level of commitment to moving forward, what would happen?
_____
_____

How would you describe your energy level right now?

Where is this energy best directed?
_____
_____
_____

If you knew that you would succeed at any thing you tried today, what would you do?
_____
_____
_____

Day 14
Evening

Date: _____   Time: _____

What did you do today that was new?

....
....

What deserves to be celebrated or acknowledged?
How did this happen?

....
....
....
....

Where did you get off track?

....
....

What are the repeating patterns of behavior that keep you from having what you want?

....
....

Anything else on your mind?

....
....

Complete this statement. Tonight I will rest peacefully knowing that...

....
....

Day 15
Morning

Date: _____   Time: _____

How do you feel right now?

....
....
....

What is driving this feeling?

....
....
....

What are you ready to release? How will this impact your life?

....
....
....

How would you describe your energy level right now?

Where is this energy best directed?

....
....
....

If you knew that you would succeed at any thing you tried today, what would you do?

....
....
....

Day 15
Evening

Date: _____ Time: _____

What did you do today that was new?

....
....

What deserves to be celebrated or acknowledged?
How did this happen?

....
....
....
....

Where did you get off track?

....
....
....

In what way have you stepped out of your comfort zone?

....
....
....

Anything else on your mind?

....
....
....

Complete this statement. Tonight I will rest peacefully
knowing that...

....
....
....

Day 16
Morning

Date: Time:

How do you feel right now?

What is driving this feeling?

What part of your Dreamcast scares you? Knowing this is likely where you need to focus your energy, what are you now ready to do?

How would you describe your energy level right now?

How would you describe your energy level right now?

Where is this energy best directed?

If you knew that you would succeed at any thing you tried today, what would you do?

Day 16
Evening

Date: _____ Time: _____

What did you do today that was new?

....
....

What deserves to be celebrated or acknowledged?
How did this happen?

....
....
....
....

Where did you get off track?

....
....

How did you expose yourself to excellence today?

....
....
....

Anything else on your mind?

....
....
....

Complete this statement. Tonight I will rest peacefully
knowing that...

....
....
....

Day 17
Morning

Date: _____   Time: _____

How do you feel right now?

....
....

What is driving this feeling?

....
....
....

Where can you find living examples of what you want for your life?

....
....
....

How would you describe your energy level right now?

Where is this energy best directed?

....
....
....

If you knew that you would succeed at any thing you tried today, what would you do?

....
....
....

Day 17
Evening

Date: _____ Time: _____

What did you do today that was new?
....
....

What deserves to be celebrated or acknowledged?
How did this happen?
....
....
....
....
....

Where did you get off track?
....
....
....

What do you notice about how you respond to challenges?
....
....
....

Anything else on your mind?
....
....
....

Complete this statement. Tonight I will rest peacefully knowing that...
....
....
....

Day 18
Morning

Date: .... Time: ....

How do you feel right now?

....
....
....

What is driving this feeling?

....
....
....

Who advocates on your behalf, even if it means holding your feet to the fire?

....
....
....
....

How would you describe your energy level right now?

Where is this energy best directed?

....
....

If you knew that you would succeed at any thing you tried today, what would you do?

....
....
....

Day 18
Evening

Date: _____ Time: _____

What did you do today that was new?

....
....

What deserves to be celebrated or acknowledged?
How did this happen?

....
....
....
....

Where did you get off track?

....
....

Describe how Day 90 will be different for you.

....
....

Anything else on your mind?

....
....

Complete this statement. Tonight I will rest peacefully
knowing that...

....
....
....

Day 19
Morning

Date: _____ Time: _____

How do you feel right now?

_____
_____
_____

What is driving this feeling?

_____
_____
_____

Let's compare the life you are creating to the one you are currently living. What doesn't align?

_____
_____
_____
_____

How would you describe your energy level right now?

Where is this energy best directed?

_____
_____
_____

If you knew that you would succeed at any thing you tried today, what would you do?

_____
_____
_____

Day 19
Evening

Date: _____   Time: _____

What did you do today that was new?

....
....

What deserves to be celebrated or acknowledged?
How did this happen?

....
....
....
....

Where did you get off track?

....
....

How will you move away from what no longer fits?

....
....

Anything else on your mind?

....
....

Complete this statement. Tonight I will rest peacefully
knowing that...

....
....

Day 20
Morning

Date: ....   Time: ....

How do you feel right now?

....
....

What is driving this feeling?

....
....
....

How does your conversation (with yourself and others), support or invalidate your beliefs and values?

....
....
....

How would you describe your energy level right now?

How would you describe your energy level right now?

Where is this energy best directed?

....
....
....

If you knew that you would succeed at any thing you tried today, what would you do?

....
....
....

Day 20
Evening

Date: ....   Time: ....

What did you do today that was new?

....

....

What did this new experience reveal about you?

....

....

....

....

Where did you get off track?

....

....

What deserves to be acknowledged or celebrated? How did this happen?

....

....

Anything else on your mind?

....

....

Complete this statement. Tonight I will rest peacefully knowing that...

....

....

Day 20 Review

A look back as you move forward Date: .... Time: ....

What stands out for you?

....
....
....
....
....

What new discoveries have surfaced for you regarding your life's direction?

....
....
....
....

In which areas of your life are you gaining traction?

....
....
....
....

Where do you notice a definite shift in your thinking?

....
....
....

Reflections and Celebrations

Date: Time:

Day 21
Morning

Date: _____ Time: _____

How do you feel right now?

_____
_____
_____

What is driving this feeling?

_____
_____
_____
_____

What changes do you want to make in order to align your vision with you current reality?

_____
_____
_____
_____

How would you describe your energy level right now?

Where is this energy best directed?

_____
_____
_____

If you knew that you would succeed at any thing you tried today, what would you do?

_____
_____
_____

Day 21
Evening

Date: _____   Time: _____

What did you do today that was new?

....

....

What deserves to be celebrated or acknowledged?
How did this happen?

....

....

....

....

Where did you get off track?

....

....

....

What will your life look like when you implement the
changes you want to make?

....

....

Anything else on your mind?

....

....

....

Complete this statement. Tonight I will rest peacefully
knowing that...

....

....

....

Day 22
Morning

Date: .... Time: ....

How do you feel right now?

....
....
....

What is driving this feeling?

....
....
....
....

What is the first step to making the changes you desire? Where will you find support with this?

....
....
....
....

How would you describe your energy level right now?

Where is this energy best directed?

....
....
....

If you knew that you would succeed at any thing you tried today, what would you do?

....
....
....

Day 22
Evening

Date: _____   Time: _____

What did you do today that was new?

....
....

What deserves to be celebrated or acknowledged?
How did this happen?

....
....
....
....

Where did you get off track?

....
....

When will you seek out the support you need?

Date ....
Time ....

Anything else on your mind?

....
....

Complete this statement. Tonight I will rest peacefully
knowing that...

....
....

Day 23
Morning

Date: .... Time: ....

How do you feel right now?

....

....

....

What is driving this feeling?

....

....

....

Which adjustments will be the most challenging?

....

....

....

....

How would you describe your energy level right now?

Where is this energy best directed?

....

....

....

If you knew that you would succeed at any thing you tried today, what would you do?

....

....

....

Day 23
Evening

Date: _____ Time: _____

What did you do today that was new?

....

....

What deserves to be celebrated or acknowledged?
How did this happen?

....

....

....

....

Where did you get off track?

....

....

....

Why are the adjustments you're making necessary?

....

....

....

Anything else on your mind?

....

....

....

Complete this statement. Tonight I will rest peacefully
knowing that...

....

....

....

Day 24
Morning

Date: .... Time: ....

How do you feel right now?

....
....
....

What is driving this feeling?

....
....
....

What visual representation do you have as a reminder of your intended direction?

....
....
....

How would you describe your energy level right now?

Where is this energy best directed?

....
....
....

If you knew that you would succeed at any thing you tried today, what would you do?

....
....
....

Day 24
Evening

Date: _____ Time: _____

What did you do today that was new?
....
....

What deserves to be celebrated or acknowledged?
How did this happen?
....
....
....
....

Where did you get off track?
....
....
....

What boundaries need to be examined?
....
....
....

Anything else on your mind?
....
....
....

Complete this statement. Tonight I will rest peacefully
knowing that...
....
....
....

Day 25
Morning

Date: _____   Time: _____

How do you feel right now?

....

....

....

What is driving this feeling?

....

....

....

How and when will you convey your new boundaries to the people who need to be aware of them?

....

....

....

How would you describe your energy level right now?

Where is this energy best directed?

....

....

....

If you knew that you would succeed at any thing you tried today, what would you do?

....

....

....

Day 25
Evening

Date: _____   Time: _____

What did you do today that was new?
....
....

What deserves to be celebrated or acknowledged?
How did this happen?
....
....
....
....

Where did you get off track?
....
....

What habits and behaviors must you leave behind in
order to get where you want to go?
....
....
....

Anything else on your mind?
....
....

Complete this statement. Tonight I will rest peacefully
knowing that...
....
....
....

Day 26
Morning

Date: _____   Time: _____

How do you feel right now?

....
....
....

What is driving this feeling?

....
....
....

What actions are you now inspired to take?

....
....
....

How would you describe your energy level right now?

Where is this energy best directed?

....
....
....

If you knew that you would succeed at any thing you tried today, what would you do?

....
....
....

Day 26
Evening

Date: _____ Time: _____

What did you do today that was new?

....

....

What deserves to be celebrated or acknowledged?
How did this happen?

....

....

....

....

Where did you get off track?

....

....

How committed are you to moving forward?

....

....

Anything else on your mind?

....

....

Complete this statement. Tonight I will rest peacefully
knowing that...

....

....

Day 27
Morning

Date: _____   Time: _____

How do you feel right now?

....

....

....

What is driving this feeling?

....

....

....

What healthy patterns of behavior have you created?

....

....

....

....

How would you describe your energy level right now?

Where is this energy best directed?

....

....

....

If you knew that you would succeed at any thing you tried today, what would you do?

....

....

....

Day 27
Evening

Date: .... Time: ....

What did you do today that was new?

....
....
....

What deserves to be celebrated or acknowledged?
How did this happen?

....
....
....
....

Where did you get off track?

....
....
....

How are you keeping track of your successes?

....
....
....

Anything else on your mind?

....
....
....

Complete this statement. Tonight I will rest peacefully
knowing that...

....
....
....

Day 28
Morning

Date: _____   Time: _____

How do you feel right now?
_____
_____
_____

What is driving this feeling?
_____
_____
_____

Why are the changes you're making so important?
_____
_____
_____
_____

How would you describe your energy level right now?

Where is this energy best directed?
_____
_____
_____

If you knew that you would succeed at any thing you tried today, what would you do?
_____
_____
_____

Day 28
Evening

Date: _____ Time: _____

What did you do today that was new?

....

....

What deserves to be celebrated or acknowledged?
How did this happen?

....

....

....

....

Where did you get off track?

....

....

....

Who will feel threatened by the changes you're
making?

....

....

Anything else on your mind?

....

....

....

Complete this statement. Tonight I will rest peacefully
knowing that...

....

....

....

Day 29
Morning

Date: _____   Time: _____

How do you feel right now?

....
....
....

What is driving this feeling?

....
....
....

How will you address the push back you are likely to receive from this forward direction?

....
....
....

How would you describe your energy level right now?

Where is this energy best directed?

....
....
....

If you knew that you would succeed at any thing you tried today, what would you do?

....
....
....

Day 29
Evening

Date: _____   Time: _____

What did you do today that was new?

_____
_____

What deserves to be celebrated or acknowledged?
How did this happen?

_____
_____
_____
_____

Where did you get off track?

_____
_____

How do the things that got you off track support your fears?

_____
_____

Anything else on your mind?

_____
_____

Complete this statement. Tonight I will rest peacefully knowing that...

_____
_____
_____

Day 30
Morning

Date: _____   Time: _____

How do you feel right now?

....
....

What is driving this feeling?

....
....
....

What additional boundaries need to be put into place to support your progress.

....
....
....

How would you describe your energy level right now?

Where is this energy best directed?

....
....

If you knew that you would succeed at any thing you tried today, what would you do?

....
....
....

Day 30
Evening

Date: _____ Time: _____

What did you do today that was new?

....
....

What deserves to be celebrated or acknowledged?
How did this happen?

....
....
....
....

Where did you get off track?

....
....
....

What areas of your life feel a bit unfamiliar?

....
....
....

Anything else on your mind?

....
....
....

Complete this statement. Tonight I will rest peacefully
knowing that...

....
....
....

Day 30 Review

A look back as you move forward Date: .... Time: ....

What stands out for you?

....
....
....
....
....

What did you make progress on? How did you do it?

....
....
....
....
....

What did you not make progress on? What happened?

....
....
....
....

What help or resources do you need in this moment?
How will you find it?

....
....
....
....

Reflections and Celebrations

Date: Time:

Day 31
Morning

Date: _____   Time: _____

How do you feel right now?

....
....
....

What is driving this feeling?

....
....
....

In what way have you boldly stepped out of your comfort zone?

....
....
....
....

How would you describe your energy level right now?

How would you describe your energy level right now?

Where is this energy best directed?

....
....
....

If you knew that you would succeed at any thing you tried today, what would you do?

....
....
....

Day 31
Evening

Date: _____   Time: _____

What did you do today that was new?

....
....

What deserves to be celebrated or acknowledged?
How did this happen?

....
....
....
....

Where did you get off track?

....
....
....

How has your response to challenges changed?

....
....
....

Anything else on your mind?

....
....
....

Complete this statement. Tonight I will rest peacefully
knowing that...

....
....
....

Day 32
Morning

How do you feel right now?

....
....

What is driving this feeling?

....
....
....

Look back at page 22. Where do you want to focus now?

....
....
....

How would you describe your energy level right now?

Where is this energy best directed?

....
....

If you knew that you would succeed at any thing you tried today, what would you do?

....
....
....

Day 32
Evening

Date: _____   Time: _____

What did you do today that was new?
....
....

What deserves to be celebrated or acknowledged?
How did this happen?
....
....
....
....

Where did you get off track?
....
....
....

When will you implement the actions to support your area of focus?
Date ....
Time ....

Anything else on your mind?
....
....

Complete this statement. Tonight I will rest peacefully knowing that...
....
....
....

Day 33
Morning

Date: _____   Time: _____

How do you feel right now?

....
....

What is driving this feeling?

....
....
....

What is the most important thing you can do today?

....
....
....

How would you describe your energy level right now?

How would you describe your energy level right now?

Where is this energy best directed?

....
....
....

If you knew that you would succeed at any thing you tried today, what would you do?

....
....
....

Day 33
Evening

Date: _____   Time: _____

What did you do today that was new?

....

....

What deserves to be celebrated or acknowledged?
How did this happen?

....

....

....

....

Where did you get off track?

....

....

How well did you do with your most important thing?

....

....

Anything else on your mind?

....

....

Complete this statement. Tonight I will rest peacefully
knowing that...

....

....

Day 34
Morning

Date: _____   Time: _____

How do you feel right now?

....
....
....

What is driving this feeling?

....
....
....

What action are you inspired to take today?

....
....
....
....

How would you describe your energy level right now?

Where is this energy best directed?

....
....
....

If you knew that you would succeed at any thing you tried today, what would you do?

....
....
....

Day 34
Evening

Date: _____   Time: _____

What did you do today that was new?

_____
_____
_____

What deserves to be celebrated or acknowledged?
How did this happen?

_____
_____
_____
_____
_____

Where did you get off track?

_____
_____
_____

Describe your thoughts about you progress so far.

_____
_____
_____

Anything else on your mind?

_____
_____
_____

Complete this statement. Tonight I will rest peacefully
knowing that...

_____
_____
_____

Day 35
Morning

Date: _____   Time: _____

How do you feel right now?

_____
_____

What is driving this feeling?

_____
_____
_____

Which habits and behaviors are no longer useful?

_____
_____
_____

How would you describe your energy level right now?

Where is this energy best directed?

_____
_____

If you knew that you would succeed at any thing you tried today, what would you do?

_____
_____
_____

Day 35
Evening

Date: .... Time: ....

What did you do today that was new?
....
....

What deserves to be celebrated or acknowledged?
How did this happen?
....
....
....
....

Where did you get off track?
....
....

What else are you ready to release?
....
....
....

Anything else on your mind?
....
....
....

Complete this statement. Tonight I will rest peacefully
knowing that...
....
....
....

Day 36
Morning

Date: _____   Time: _____

How do you feel right now?

....
....
....

What is driving this feeling?

....
....
....

How can you carry your feelings of accomplishment forward?

....
....
....

How would you describe your energy level right now?

Where is this energy best directed?

....
....
....

If you knew that you would succeed at any thing you tried today, what would you do?

....
....
....

Day 36
Evening

Date: _____   Time: _____

What did you do today that was new?

....
....

What deserves to be celebrated or acknowledged?
How did this happen?

....
....
....
....

Where did you get off track?

....
....
....

How committed are you to moving forward?

....
....
....

Anything else on your mind?

....
....
....

Complete this statement. Tonight I will rest peacefully
knowing that...

....
....
....

Day 37
Morning

Date: _____   Time: _____

How do you feel right now?

....
....
....

What is driving this feeling?

....
....
....

What other healthy patterns of behavior have you created?

....
....
....
....

How would you describe your energy level right now?

Where is this energy best directed?

....
....
....

If you knew that you would succeed at any thing you tried today, what would you do?

....
....
....

Day 37
Evening

Date: _____ Time: _____

What did you do today that was new?

_____
_____

What deserves to be celebrated or acknowledged?
How did this happen?

_____
_____
_____
_____

Where did you get off track?

_____
_____
_____

When was the last time you took a real day off? When
is your next one?

_____
_____

Anything else on your mind?

_____
_____
_____

Complete this statement. Tonight I will rest peacefully
knowing that...

_____
_____
_____

Day 38
Morning

Date: Time:

How do you feel right now?

....

....

....

What is driving this feeling?

....

....

....

Who else is noticing your change in perspective?

....

....

....

....

How would you describe your energy level right now?

Where is this energy best directed?

....

....

....

If you knew that you would succeed at any thing you tried today, what would you do?

....

....

....

Day 38
Evening

Date: _____   Time: _____

What did you do today that was new?

....
....
....

What deserves to be celebrated or acknowledged?
How did this happen?

....
....
....
....
....

Where did you get off track?

....
....
....

Who will feel threatened by the changes you're
making?

....
....
....

Anything else on your mind?

....
....
....

Complete this statement. Tonight I will rest peacefully
knowing that...

....
....
....

Day 39
Morning

How do you feel right now?

....
....
....

What is driving this feeling?

....
....
....

How will you address the push back you are likely to receive from this forward direction?

....
....
....

How would you describe your energy level right now?

Where is this energy best directed?

....
....

If you knew that you would succeed at any thing you tried today, what would you do?

....
....
....

Day 39
Evening

Date: _____   Time: _____

What did you do today that was new?
....
....

What deserves to be celebrated or acknowledged?
How did this happen?
....
....
....
....
....

Where did you get off track?
....
....
....

How have your adjusted boundaries been working?
....
....
....

Anything else on your mind?
....
....
....

Complete this statement. Tonight I will rest peacefully
knowing that...
....
....
....

Day 40
Morning

Date: _____   Time: _____

How do you feel right now?

....
....
....

What is driving this feeling?

....
....
....

What additional boundaries need to be put into place to support your progress.

....
....
....

How would you describe your energy level right now?

Where is this energy best directed?

....
....

If you knew that you would succeed at any thing you tried today, what would you do?

....
....
....

Day 40
Evening

Date: _____ Time: _____

What did you do today that was new?

....
....

What deserves to be celebrated or acknowledged?
How did this happen?

....
....
....
....

Where did you get off track?

....
....

How has your life changed since beginning this
journey?

....
....

Anything else on your mind?

....
....

Complete this statement. Tonight I will rest peacefully
knowing that...

....
....
....

Day 40 Review

A look back as you move forward Date: _____ Time: _____

What stands out for you?

_____
_____
_____
_____
_____

What did you make progress on? How did you do it?

_____
_____
_____
_____
_____

What did you not make progress on? What happened?

_____
_____
_____
_____
_____

What do you need to maintain your progress?

_____
_____
_____
_____

Reflections and Celebrations

Date:

Time:

Day 41
Morning

Date: .... Time: ....

How do you feel right now?

....

....

What is driving this feeling?

....

....

....

What obstacles or challenges have surfaced?

....

....

....

....

How would you describe your energy level right now?

Where is this energy best directed?

....

....

....

If you knew that you would succeed at any thing you tried today, what would you do?

....

....

....

Day 41
Evening

Date: _____ Time: _____

What did you do today that was new?

....

....

What deserves to be celebrated or acknowledged?
How did this happen?

....

....

....

....

Where did you get off track?

....

....

How did you infuse joy into your day?

....

....

Anything else on your mind?

....

....

Complete this statement. Tonight I will rest peacefully
knowing that...

....

....

Day 42
Morning

Date: _____   Time: _____

How do you feel right now?

....
....
....

What is driving this feeling?

....
....
....

Are the new obstacles/challenges, something you actually see or believe to be present?

....
....
....

How would you describe your energy level right now?

Where is this energy best directed?

....
....

If you knew that you would succeed at any thing you tried today, what would you do?

....
....
....

Day 42
Evening

Date: _____ Time: _____

What did you do today that was new?

....
....

What deserves to be celebrated or acknowledged?
How did this happen?

....
....
....
....

Where did you get off track?

....
....
....

How do you address adversity?

....
....
....

Anything else on your mind?

....
....
....

Complete this statement. Tonight I will rest peacefully
knowing that...

....
....
....

Day 43
Morning

Date: Time:

How do you feel right now?

....

....

What is driving this feeling?

....

....

....

How has your conversation changed?

....

....

....

How would you describe your energy level right now?

Where is this energy best directed?

....

....

....

If you knew that you would succeed at any thing you tried today, what would you do?

....

....

....

Day 43
Evening

Date: _____ Time: _____

What did you do today that was new?

....
....

What deserves to be celebrated or acknowledged?
How did this happen?

....
....
....
....

Where did you get off track?

....
....

Where are you feeling unfulfilled?

....
....
....

Anything else on your mind?

....
....
....

Complete this statement. Tonight I will rest peacefully
knowing that...

....
....
....

Day 44
Morning

Date: _____   Time: _____

How do you feel right now?
....
....
....

What is driving this feeling?
....
....
....

What vision supporting activity will you do today?

....
....
....

How would you describe your energy level right now?

Where is this energy best directed?
....
....
....

If you knew that you would succeed at any thing you tried today, what would you do?
....
....
....

Day 44
Evening

Date: _____ Time: _____

What did you do today that was new?

_____

_____

What deserves to be celebrated or acknowledged?
How did this happen?

_____

_____

_____

_____

Where did you get off track?

_____

_____

How did your vision supporting activity go?

_____

_____

Anything else on your mind?

_____

_____

Complete this statement. Tonight I will rest peacefully
knowing that...

_____

_____

Day 45
Morning

Date: _____   Time: _____

How do you feel right now?

....
....
....

What is driving this feeling?

....
....
....

How well does your daily schedule align with your intentions?

....
....
....

How would you describe your energy level right now?

How well does your daily schedule align with your energy level right now?

Where is this energy best directed?

....
....
....

If you knew that you would succeed at any thing you tried today, what would you do?

....
....
....

Day 45
Evening

Date: _____   Time: _____

What did you do today that was new?

_____
_____
_____

What deserves to be celebrated or acknowledged?
How did this happen?

_____
_____
_____
_____
_____

Where did you get off track?

_____
_____
_____

What might be the benefits of having your schedule
and your intentions in alignment?

_____
_____
_____
_____

Anything else on your mind?

_____
_____
_____

Complete this statement. Tonight I will rest peacefully
knowing that...

_____
_____
_____

Day 46
Morning

Date: _____ Time: _____

How do you feel right now?

....

....

What is driving this feeling?

....

....

If you could design your perfect day what would it look like?

....

....

....

How would you describe your energy level right now?

How would you describe your energy level right now?

Where is this energy best directed?

....

....

If you knew that you would succeed at any thing you tried today, what would you do?

....

....

....

Day 46
Evening

Date: _____   Time: _____

What did you do today that was new?

_____
_____

What deserves to be celebrated or acknowledged?
How did this happen?

_____
_____
_____
_____

Where did you get off track?

_____
_____

What happened the last time you put yourself first?

_____
_____

Anything else on your mind?

_____
_____

Complete this statement. Tonight I will rest peacefully
knowing that...

_____
_____

Day 47
Morning

Date: _____   Time: _____

How do you feel right now?

....
....
....

What is driving this feeling?

....
....
....

What is your most important activity today?

....
....
....

How would you describe your energy level right now?

How would you describe your energy level right now?

Where is this energy best directed?

....
....
....

If you knew that you would succeed at any thing you tried today, what would you do?

....
....
....

Day 47
Evening

Date: Time:

What did you do today that was new?

What deserves to be celebrated or acknowledged? How did this happen?

Where did you get off track?

How did you do with your most important activity?

Anything else on your mind?

Complete this statement. Tonight I will rest peacefully knowing that...

Day 48
Morning

Date: Time:

How do you feel right now?

....

....

....

What is driving this feeling?

....

....

....

In what areas of your life are you thriving?

....

....

....

How would you describe your energy level right now?

Where is this energy best directed?

....

....

....

If you knew that you would succeed at any thing you tried today, what would you do?

....

....

....

Day 48
Evening

Date: _____ Time: _____

What did you do today that was new?

_____
_____

What deserves to be celebrated or acknowledged?
How did this happen?

_____
_____
_____
_____

Where did you get off track?

_____
_____

What has been the main reason for your progress?

_____
_____

Anything else on your mind?

_____
_____

Complete this statement. Tonight I will rest peacefully
knowing that...

_____
_____

Day 49
Morning

Date: _____ Time: _____

How do you feel right now?

_____
_____

What is driving this feeling?

_____
_____
_____

What has not been addressed?

_____
_____
_____

How would you describe your energy level right now?

Where is this energy best directed?

_____
_____

If you knew that you would succeed at any thing you tried today, what would you do?

_____
_____

Day 49
Evening

Date: _____   Time: _____

What did you do today that was new?

....
....

What deserves to be celebrated or acknowledged?
How did this happen?

....
....
....
....

Where did you get off track?

....
....

How are you feeding yourself emotionally? Spiritually?

....
....
....

Anything else on your mind?

....
....
....

Complete this statement. Tonight I will rest peacefully
knowing that...

....
....

Day 50
Morning

Date: _____ Time: _____

How do you feel right now?
....
....
....

What is driving this feeling?
....
....
....

What action are you inspired to take today?

....
....
....

How would you describe your energy level right now?

Where is this energy best directed?
....
....
....

If you knew that you would succeed at any thing you tried today, what would you do?
....
....
....

Day 50
Evening

Date: Time:

What did you do today that was new?

....
....

What deserves to be celebrated or acknowledged?
How did this happen?

....
....
....
....

Where did you get off track?

....
....

How did you expose yourself to excellence today?

....
....

Anything else on your mind?

....
....

Complete this statement. Tonight I will rest peacefully
knowing that...

....
....

Day 50 Review

A look back as you move forward Date: _____ Time: _____

Let's look back at the things you intended to implement as a result of your dreamcasting.

What, if anything, has changed?

_____
_____
_____
_____
_____
_____

What needs to be addressed and implemented?
Date and time you will get this going.

_____
_____
_____
_____

What support do you need to make this happen?
When will you ask for this support?

_____
_____

How will you get going if you must do it alone?

_____
_____
_____

Reflections and Celebrations

Date:

Time:

Day 51
Morning

Date: Time:

How do you feel right now?

....
....
....

What is driving this feeling?

....
....
....

What are your guiding principles and values?

....
....
....

How would you describe your energy level right now?

Where is this energy best directed?

....
....
....

If you knew that you would succeed at any thing you tried today, what would you do?

....
....
....

Day 51
Evening

Date: Time:

What did you do today that was new?

....
....

What deserves to be celebrated or acknowledged?
How did this happen?

....
....
....
....

Where did you get off track?

....
....
....

How did you expose yourself to excellence today?

....
....
....

Anything else on your mind?

....
....
....

Complete this statement. Tonight I will rest peacefully
knowing that...

....
....
....

Day 52
Morning

How do you feel right now?

....

....

What is driving this feeling?

....

....

....

How do you demonstrate your guiding principles
and values daily?

....

....

....

How would you describe your energy level right now?

Where is this energy best directed?

....

....

....

If you knew that you would succeed at any thing you
tried today, what would you do?

....

....

....

Day 52
Evening

Date: .... Time: ....

What did you do today that was new?

....
....

What deserves to be celebrated or acknowledged?
How did this happen?

....
....
....
....

Where did you get off track?

....
....
....

How did you expose yourself to excellence today?

....
....
....

Anything else on your mind?

....
....
....

Complete this statement. Tonight I will rest peacefully
knowing that...

....
....
....

Day 53
Morning

Date: _____   Time: _____

How do you feel right now?
....
....
....

What is driving this feeling?
....
....
....

What do you hope for?
....
....
....

How would you describe your energy level right now?

Where is this energy best directed?
....
....

If you knew that you would succeed at any thing you tried today, what would you do?
....
....

Day 53
Evening

Date: _____ Time: _____

What did you do today that was new?

....

....

What did this new experience reveal about you?

....

....

Where did you get off track?

....

....

What deserves to be celebrated or acknowledged?
How did this happen?

....

....

....

....

Anything else on your mind?

....

....

....

Complete this statement. Tonight I will rest peacefully
knowing that...

....

....

Day 54
Morning

Date: _____   Time: _____

How do you feel right now?

....
....
....

What is driving this feeling?

....
....
....

How do you want people to experience you today?

....
....
....

How would you describe your energy level right now?

Where is this energy best directed?

....
....
....

If you knew that you would succeed at any thing you tried today, what would you do?

....
....
....

Day 54
Evening

Date: _____ Time: _____

What did you do today that was new?

_____
_____

What did this new experience reveal about you?

_____
_____
_____

Where did you get off track?

_____
_____

What deserves to be celebrated or acknowledged?
How did this happen?

_____
_____
_____
_____

Anything else on your mind?

_____
_____
_____

Complete this statement. Tonight I will rest peacefully
knowing that...

_____
_____
_____

Day 55
Morning

Date: _____   Time: _____

How do you feel right now?

....
....

What is driving this feeling?

....
....
....

What do you want MORE of in your life?

....
....
....

How would you describe your energy level right now?

Where is this energy best directed?

....
....
....

If you knew that you would succeed at any thing you tried today, what would you do?

....
....

Day 55
Evening

Date: Time:

What did you do today that was new?

....

....

What deserves to be celebrated or acknowledged?
How did this happen?

....

....

....

....

Where did you get off track?

....

....

Describe what you want to move towards.

....

....

Anything else on your mind?

....

....

Complete this statement. Tonight I will rest peacefully
knowing that...

....

....

Day 56
Morning

Date: _____   Time: _____

How do you feel right now?

....

....

....

What is driving this feeling?

....

....

....

What do you want LESS of in your life?

....

....

....

....

How would you describe your energy level right now?

Where is this energy best directed?

....

....

....

If you knew that you would succeed at any thing you tried today, what would you do?

....

....

....

Day 56
Evening

Date: _____ Time: _____

What did you do today that was new?
....
....

What deserves to be celebrated or acknowledged?
How did this happen?
....
....
....
....

Where did you get off track?
....
....
....

Describe what you want to move away from.
....
....
....

Anything else on your mind?
....
....

Complete this statement. Tonight I will rest peacefully
knowing that...
....
....
....

Day 57
Morning

Date: _____   Time: _____

How do you feel right now?

....
....

What is driving this feeling?

....
....

Describe the roles you now play in your life. What is different from before?

....
....
....

How would you describe your energy level right now?

Where is this energy best directed?

....
....

If you knew that you would succeed at any thing you tried today, what would you do?

....
....

Day 57
Evening

Date: _____   Time: _____

What did you do today that was new?

....
....

What deserves to be celebrated or acknowledged?
How did this happen?

....
....
....
....

Where did you get off track?

....
....
....

Describe your feelings about the roles you play.

....
....
....

Anything else on your mind?

....
....
....

Complete this statement. Tonight I will rest peacefully
knowing that...

....
....

Day 58
Morning

How do you feel right now?

....

....

....

What is driving this feeling?

....

....

....

How do your life's roles influence how you spend your time? What is different from before?

....

....

....

How would you describe your energy level right now?

Where is this energy best directed?

....

....

....

If you knew that you would succeed at any thing you tried today, what would you do?

....

....

....

Day 58
Evening

Date: .... Time: ....

What did you do today that was new?

....
....

What deserves to be celebrated or acknowledged?
How did this happen?

....
....
....
....

Where did you get off track?

....
....
....

How does your daily routine align with what you want?

....
....
....

Anything else on your mind?

....
....

Complete this statement. Tonight I will rest peacefully
knowing that...

....
....
....

Day 59
Morning

Date: _____   Time: _____

How do you feel right now?

....
....
....

What is driving this feeling?

....
....
....

What brings you joy?

....
....
....

How would you describe your energy level right now?

Where is this energy best directed?

....
....

If you knew that you would succeed at any thing you tried today, what would you do?

....
....
....

Day 59
Evening

Date: _____ Time: _____

What did you do today that was new?

....
....

What deserves to be celebrated or acknowledged?
How did this happen?

....
....
....
....

Where did you get off track?

....
....
....

How did you infuse joy into your day?

....
....
....

Anything else on your mind?

....
....
....

Complete this statement. Tonight I will rest peacefully
knowing that...

....
....

Day 60
Morning

Date: _____ Time: _____

How do you feel right now?

....

....

What is driving this feeling?

....

....

What do you have a non-negotiable commitment to? Who benefits from this?

....

....

....

How would you describe your energy level right now?

Where is this energy best directed?

....

....

If you knew that you would succeed at any thing you tried today, what would you do?

....

....

....

Day 60
Evening

Date: _____   Time: _____

What did you do today that was new?

....

....

What deserves to be celebrated or acknowledged?
How did this happen?

....

....

....

....

Where did you get off track?

....

....

....

What does self-care look like for you?

....

....

....

Anything else on your mind?

....

....

....

Complete this statement. Tonight I will rest peacefully
knowing that...

....

....

Day 60 Review

A look back as you move forward   Date: _____   Time: _____

What stands out for you?

_____
_____
_____
_____

What did you make progress on? How did you do it?

_____
_____
_____
_____

What did you not make progress on? What happened?

_____
_____
_____
_____

What are you tired of hearing yourself say?

_____
_____
_____
_____

Reflections and Celebrations

Date:

Time:

Day 61
Morning

Date: _____   Time: _____

How do you feel right now?
....
....
....

What is driving this feeling?
....
....
....

What changes do you want to make?
....
....
....
....

How would you describe your energy level right now?

Where is this energy best directed?
....
....
....

If you knew that you would succeed at any thing you tried today, what would you do?
....
....
....

Day 61
Evening

Date: Time:

What did you do today that was new?

What deserves to be celebrated or acknowledged?
How did this happen?

Where did you get off track?

What will your life look like when you implement the
changes you want to make?

Anything else on your mind?

Complete this statement. Tonight I will rest peacefully
knowing that...

Day 62
Morning

Date: _____   Time: _____

How do you feel right now?

....

....

What is driving this feeling?

....

....

....

What is the first step to making the changes you want to make? Where will you find support?

....

....

....

....

How would you describe your energy level right now?

Where is this energy best directed?

....

....

If you knew that you would succeed at any thing you tried today, what would you do?

....

....

....

Day 62
Evening

Date: _____   Time: _____

What did you do today that was new?

....
....

What deserves to be celebrated or acknowledged?
How did this happen?

....
....
....
....

Where did you get off track?

....
....

When will you seek out the support you need?

Date ....
Time ....

Anything else on your mind?

....
....

Complete this statement. Tonight I will rest peacefully
knowing that...

....
....

Day 63
Morning

Date: _____   Time: _____

How do you feel right now?

....
....

What is driving this feeling?

....
....
....

Which adjustments will be the most challenging?

....
....

How would you describe your energy level right now?

Where is this energy best directed?

....
....
....

If you knew that you would succeed at any thing you tried today, what would you do?

....
....
....

Day 63
Evening

Date: Time:

What did you do today that was new?

....

....

What deserves to be celebrated or acknowledged?
How did this happen?

....

....

....

....

Where did you get off track?

....

....

Why are the adjustments you're making necessary?

....

....

Anything else on your mind?

....

....

Complete this statement. Tonight I will rest peacefully knowing that...

....

....

Day 64
Morning

Date: _____   Time: _____

How do you feel right now?

....
....
....

What is driving this feeling?

....
....
....

What visual representation do you have as a reminder of your intended direction?

....
....
....

How would you describe your energy level right now?

Where is this energy best directed?

....
....
....

If you knew that you would succeed at any thing you tried today, what would you do?

....
....
....

Day 64
Evening

Date: _____ Time: _____

What did you do today that was new?

....
....

What deserves to be celebrated or acknowledged?
How did this happen?

....
....
....
....
....

Where did you get off track?

....
....

What boundaries need to be examined?

....
....

Anything else on your mind?

....
....

Complete this statement. Tonight I will rest peacefully
knowing that...

....
....

Day 65
Morning

How do you feel right now?

....

....

What is driving this feeling?

....

....

....

How and when will you convey your new boundaries to the people who need to be aware of them?

....

....

....

How would you describe your energy level right now?

Where is this energy best directed?

....

....

If you knew that you would succeed at any thing you tried today, what would you do?

....

....

....

Day 65
Evening

Date: _____ Time: _____

What did you do today that was new?

_____

_____

What deserves to be celebrated or acknowledged? How did this happen?

_____

_____

_____

Where did you get off track?

_____

_____

What habits and behaviors must you leave behind in order to continue your progress?

_____

_____

Anything else on your mind?

_____

_____

Complete this statement. Tonight I will rest peacefully knowing that...

_____

_____

Day 66
Morning

Date: _____   Time: _____

How do you feel right now?

....
....

What is driving this feeling?

....
....
....

What actions are you now inspired to take?

....
....
....

How would you describe your energy level right now?

How would you describe your energy level right now?

Where is this energy best directed?

....
....
....

If you knew that you would succeed at any thing you tried today, what would you do?

....
....

Day 66
Evening

Date: Time:

What did you do today that was new?

What deserves to be celebrated or acknowledged? How did this happen?

Where did you get off track?

How committed are you to moving forward?

Anything else on your mind?

Complete this statement. Tonight I will rest peacefully knowing that...

Day 67
Morning

Date: _____   Time: _____

How do you feel right now?

_____
_____
_____

What is driving this feeling?

_____
_____
_____

What healthy patterns of behavior are you now implementing?

_____
_____
_____

How would you describe your energy level right now?

Where is this energy best directed?

_____
_____
_____

If you knew that you would succeed at any thing you tried today, what would you do?

_____
_____
_____

Day 67
Evening

Date: _____   Time: _____

What did you do today that was new?

....

....

What deserves to be celebrated or acknowledged?
How did this happen?

....

....

....

....

Where did you get off track?

....

....

How are you keeping account of your successes?

....

....

....

Anything else on your mind?

....

....

Complete this statement. Tonight I will rest peacefully
knowing that...

....

....

Day 68
Morning

Date: _____   Time: _____

How do you feel right now?

_____
_____
_____

What is driving this feeling?

_____
_____
_____

Why are the changes you're making so important?

_____
_____
_____
_____

How would you describe your energy level right now?

Where is this energy best directed?

_____
_____
_____

If you knew that you would succeed at any thing you tried today, what would you do?

_____
_____
_____

Day 68
Evening

Date: _____ Time: _____

What did you do today that was new?

....

....

What deserves to be celebrated or acknowledged?
How did this happen?

....

....

....

....

Where did you get off track?

....

....

Who will feel threatened by the changes you're
making?

....

....

Anything else on your mind?

....

....

Complete this statement. Tonight I will rest peacefully
knowing that...

....

....

Day 69
Morning

Date: _____   Time: _____

How do you feel right now?

....

....

What is driving this feeling?

....

....

How will you address the push back you are likely to receive from this forward direction?

....

....

....

How would you describe your energy level right now?

Where is this energy best directed?

....

....

If you knew that you would succeed at any thing you tried today, what would you do?

....

....

....

Day 69
Evening

Date: _____   Time: _____

What did you do today that was new?

....
....

What deserves to be celebrated or acknowledged?
How did this happen?

....
....
....
....

Where did you get off track?

....
....
....

How do you know that NOW is the right time for the changes you will make?

....
....

Anything else on your mind?

....
....

Complete this statement. Tonight I will rest peacefully knowing that...

....
....

Day 70
Morning

Date: _____   Time: _____

How do you feel right now?

....
....
....

What is driving this feeling?

....
....
....

What additional boundaries need to be put into place to support your progress.

....
....
....

How would you describe your energy level right now?

Where is this energy best directed?

....
....
....

If you knew that you would succeed at any thing you tried today, what would you do?

....
....
....

Day 70
Evening

Date: _____   Time: _____

What did you do today that was new?

_____
_____

What deserves to be celebrated or acknowledged?
How did this happen?

_____
_____
_____
_____

Where did you get off track?

_____
_____
_____

What areas of your life feel a bit unfamiliar?

_____
_____
_____

Anything else on your mind?

_____
_____
_____

Complete this statement. Tonight I will rest peacefully
knowing that...

_____
_____
_____

Day 70 Review

A look back as you move forward Date: _____ Time: _____

What stands out for you?

_____
_____
_____
_____
_____

What did you make progress on? How did you do it?

_____
_____
_____
_____
_____

What did you not make progress on? What happened?

_____
_____
_____
_____
_____

What would you like to happen in the next 10 days?

_____
_____
_____
_____

Reflections and Celebrations

Date: Time:

Day 71
Morning

Date: _____   Time: _____

How do you feel right now?

_____
_____
_____

What is driving this feeling?

_____
_____
_____
_____

What do you want?

_____
_____
_____
_____

How would you describe your energy level right now?

Where is this energy best directed?

_____
_____
_____

If you knew that you would succeed at any thing you tried today, what would you do?

_____
_____
_____

Day 71
Evening

Date: Time:

What did you do today that was new?

What deserves to be celebrated or acknowledged? How did this happen?

Where did you get off track?

How will you get what you want?

Anything else on your mind?

Complete this statement. Tonight I will rest peacefully knowing that...

Day 72
Morning

Date: _____   Time: _____

How do you feel right now?

....
....
....

What is driving this feeling?

....
....
....

Who else knows about your vision? Why did you tell them?

....
....
....

How would you describe your energy level right now?

How would you describe your energy level right now?

Where is this energy best directed?

....
....
....

If you knew that you would succeed at any thing you tried today, what would you do?

....
....
....

Day 72
Evening

Date: Time:

What did you do today that was new?

....

....

What deserves to be celebrated or acknowledged?
How did this happen?

....

....

....

....

Where did you get off track?

....

....

....

How did you expose yourself to excellence today?

....

....

....

Anything else on your mind?

....

....

....

Complete this statement. Tonight I will rest peacefully
knowing that...

....

....

....

Day 73
Morning

Date: _____   Time: _____

How do you feel right now?

....

....

....

What is driving this feeling?

....

....

....

Why do you deserve to have your vision become reality?

....

....

....

How would you describe your energy level right now?

Where is this energy best directed?

....

....

....

If you knew that you would succeed at any thing you tried today, what would you do?

....

....

....

Day 73
Evening

Date: _____ Time: _____

What did you do today that was new?

_____
_____

What did this new experience reveal about you?

_____
_____

Where did you get off track?

_____
_____

What deserves to be celebrated or acknowledged? How did this happen?

_____
_____
_____
_____

Anything else on your mind?

_____
_____
_____

Complete this statement. Tonight I will rest peacefully knowing that...

_____
_____
_____

Day 74
Morning

Date: _____   Time: _____

How do you feel right now?

_____
_____
_____

What is driving this feeling?

_____
_____
_____

How do you want people to experience you today?

_____
_____
_____

How would you describe your energy level right now?

Where is this energy best directed?

_____
_____
_____

If you knew that you would succeed at any thing you tried today, what would you do?

_____
_____

Day 74
Evening

Date: Time:

What did you do today that was new?

What did this new experience reveal about you?

Where did you get off track?

What deserves to be celebrated or acknowledged?
How did this happen?

Anything else on your mind?

Complete this statement. Tonight I will rest peacefully
knowing that...

Day 75
Morning

Date: _____   Time: _____

How do you feel right now?

....

....

....

What is driving this feeling?

....

....

....

What do you want MORE of ?

....

....

....

How would you describe your energy level right now?

Where is this energy best directed?

....

....

....

If you knew that you would succeed at any thing you tried today, what would you do?

....

....

....

Day 75
Evening

Date: Time:

What did you do today that was new?

What deserves to be celebrated or acknowledged?
How did this happen?

Where did you get off track?

Describe what you want to move towards.

Anything else on your mind?

Complete this statement. Tonight I will rest peacefully
knowing that...

Day 76
Morning

Date: _____   Time: _____

How do you feel right now?
....
....
....

What is driving this feeling?
....
....
....

What do you want LESS of ?
....
....
....

How would you describe your energy level right now?

Where is this energy best directed?
....
....
....

If you knew that you would succeed at any thing you tried today, what would you do?
....
....
....

Day 76
Evening

Date: Time:

What did you do today that was new?

What deserves to be celebrated or acknowledged?
How did this happen?

Where did you get off track?

Describe what you want to move away from.

Anything else on your mind?

Complete this statement. Tonight I will rest peacefully
knowing that...

Day 77
Morning

Date: _____   Time: _____

How do you feel right now?

....

....

What is driving this feeling?

....

....

....

Who shares your vision?

....

....

....

How would you describe your energy level right now?

Where is this energy best directed?

....

....

....

If you knew that you would succeed at any thing you tried today, what would you do?

....

....

....

Day 77
Evening

Date: Time:

What did you do today that was new?

....
....
....

What deserves to be celebrated or acknowledged?
How did this happen?

....
....
....
....
....

Where did you get off track?

....
....
....

Why do you deserve to have what you want?

....
....
....

Anything else on your mind?

....
....
....

Complete this statement. Tonight I will rest peacefully
knowing that...

....
....
....

Day 78
Morning

Date: _____   Time: _____

How do you feel right now?

....

....

....

What is driving this feeling?

....

....

....

Who is no longer a proper fit for your inner circle?

....

....

....

How would you describe your energy level right now?

Where is this energy best directed?

....

....

....

If you knew that you would succeed at any thing you tried today, what would you do?

....

....

....

Day 78
Evening

Date: Time:

What did you do today that was new?

....
....

What deserves to be celebrated or acknowledged?
How did this happen?

....
....
....
....

Where did you get off track?

....
....

How will you address the adjustment to your inner
circle?

....
....

Anything else on your mind?

....
....

Complete this statement. Tonight I will rest peacefully
knowing that...

....
....

Day 79
Morning

Date: _____   Time: _____

How do you feel right now?

_____

_____

_____

What is driving this feeling?

_____

_____

_____

What feels like a WIN right now?

_____

_____

_____

_____

How would you describe your energy level right now?

Where is this energy best directed?

_____

_____

_____

If you knew that you would succeed at any thing you tried today, what would you do?

_____

_____

_____

Day 79
Evening

Date: _____   Time: _____

What did you do today that was new?

....
....

What deserves to be celebrated or acknowledged?
How did this happen?

....
....
....
....

Where did you get off track?

....
....
....

What practices have you put in place to duplicate
your WINs?

....
....

Anything else on your mind?

....
....
....

Complete this statement. Tonight I will rest peacefully
knowing that...

....
....
....

Day 80
Morning

Date: _____   Time: _____

How do you feel right now?

_____

_____

_____

What is driving this feeling?

_____

_____

_____

Who is the first person you call when something great happens? Why is this?

_____

_____

_____

How would you describe your energy level right now?

Where is this energy best directed?

_____

_____

_____

If you knew that you would succeed at any thing you tried today, what would you do?

_____

_____

_____

Day 80
Evening

Date: _____   Time: _____

What did you do today that was new?

....
....

What deserves to be celebrated or acknowledged?
How did this happen?

....
....
....
....

Where did you get off track?

....
....
....

What habits are you holding onto that no longer serve
you?

....
....

Anything else on your mind?

....
....

Complete this statement. Tonight I will rest peacefully
knowing that...

....
....
....

Day 80 Review

A look back as you move forward Date: _____ Time: _____

This is our final 10-day period so let's make it count!

What feelings and actions are in alignment with where you are going?

....
....
....
....
....
....

How will you continue this?

....
....
....

What feelings and actions do not align with your direction and need to be changed or eliminated?

....
....
....
....

How will you address this?

....
....
....

Reflections and Celebrations

Date: Time:

Day 81
Morning

Date: _____   Time: _____

How do you feel right now?

....

....

....

What is driving this feeling?

....

....

....

What changes do you want to make?

....

....

....

How would you describe your energy level right now?

Where is this energy best directed?

....

....

If you knew that you would succeed at any thing you tried today, what would you do?

....

....

....

Day 81
Evening

Date: Time:

What did you do today that was new?

....
....
....

What deserves to be celebrated or acknowledged?
How did this happen?

....
....
....
....

Where did you get off track?

....
....
....

What will your life look like when you implement the
changes you want to make?

....
....
....

Anything else on your mind?

....
....
....

Complete this statement. Tonight I will rest peacefully
knowing that...

....
....
....

Day 82
Morning

Date: _____   Time: _____

How do you feel right now?

_____
_____
_____

What is driving this feeling?

_____
_____
_____

What is the first step to making the changes you want to make? Where will you find support?

_____
_____
_____
_____

How would you describe your energy level right now?

Where is this energy best directed?

_____
_____
_____

If you knew that you would succeed at any thing you tried today, what would you do?

_____
_____
_____

Day 82
Evening

Date: _____   Time: _____

What did you do today that was new?

_____
_____

What deserves to be celebrated or acknowledged?
How did this happen?

_____
_____
_____
_____

Where did you get off track?

_____
_____

When will you seek out the support you need?

Date _____
Time _____

Anything else on your mind?

_____
_____

Complete this statement. Tonight I will rest peacefully
knowing that...

_____
_____
_____

Day 83
Morning

Date: _____   Time: _____

How do you feel right now?

....

....

What is driving this feeling?

....

....

....

Which adjustments will be the most challenging?

....

....

....

How would you describe your energy level right now?

Where is this energy best directed?

....

....

If you knew that you would succeed at any thing you tried today, what would you do?

....

....

....

Day 83
Evening

Date: _____   Time: _____

What did you do today that was new?

_____

_____

What deserves to be celebrated or acknowledged?
How did this happen?

_____

_____

_____

_____

Where did you get off track?

_____

_____

Why are the adjustments you're making necessary?

_____

_____

Anything else on your mind?

_____

_____

Complete this statement. Tonight I will rest peacefully
knowing that...

_____

_____

Day 84
Morning

Date: _____   Time: _____

How do you feel right now?

....

....

....

What is driving this feeling?

....

....

....

What visual representation do you have as a reminder of your intended direction?

....

....

....

How would you describe your energy level right now?

Where is this energy best directed?

....

....

....

If you knew that you would succeed at any thing you tried today, what would you do?

....

....

....

Day 84
Evening

Date: _____   Time: _____

What did you do today that was new?

....
....

What deserves to be celebrated or acknowledged?
How did this happen?

....
....
....
....

Where did you get off track?

....
....
....

What boundaries need to be re- examined?

....
....
....

Anything else on your mind?

....
....

Complete this statement. Tonight I will rest peacefully
knowing that...

....
....
....

Day 85
Morning

Date: _____   Time: _____

How do you feel right now?

....
....

What is driving this feeling?

....
....
....

How and when will you convey your new boundaries
to the people who need to be aware of them?

....
....
....

How would you describe your energy level right now?

Where is this energy best directed?

....
....
....

If you knew that you would succeed at any thing you
tried today, what would you do?

....
....
....

Day 85
Evening

Date: Time:

What did you do today that was new?

....
....

What deserves to be celebrated or acknowledged?
How did this happen?

....
....
....
....

Where did you get off track?

....
....

What habits and behaviors must you leave behind in
order to get where you want to go?

....
....
....

Anything else on your mind?

....
....

Complete this statement. Tonight I will rest peacefully
knowing that...

....
....

Day 86
Morning

Date: _____ Time: _____

How do you feel right now?

....
....
....

What is driving this feeling?

....
....
....

What actions are you now inspired to take?

....
....
....

How would you describe your energy level right now?

Where is this energy best directed?

....
....
....

If you knew that you would succeed at any thing you tried today, what would you do?

....
....
....

Day 86
Evening

Date: Time:

What did you do today that was new?

....
....

What deserves to be celebrated or acknowledged?
How did this happen?

....
....
....
....

Where did you get off track?

....
....

How committed are you to moving forward?

....
....
....

Anything else on your mind?

....
....

Complete this statement. Tonight I will rest peacefully
knowing that...

....
....

Day 87
Morning

Date: Time:

How do you feel right now?

....

....

....

What is driving this feeling?

....

....

....

What healthy patterns of behavior have you created?

....

....

....

....

How would you describe your energy level right now?

How is this energy best directed?

Where is this energy best directed?

....

....

If you knew that you would succeed at any thing you tried today, what would you do?

....

....

....

Day 87
Evening

Date: Time:

What did you do today that was new?

What deserves to be celebrated or acknowledged?
How did this happen?

Where did you get off track?

How are you keeping account of your successes?

Anything else on your mind?

Complete this statement. Tonight I will rest peacefully
knowing that...

Day 88
Morning

Date: _____   Time: _____

How do you feel right now?

....
....
....

What is driving this feeling?

....
....
....

Why are the changes you're making so important?

....
....
....

How would you describe your energy level right now?

Where is this energy best directed?

....
....
....

If you knew that you would succeed at any thing you tried today, what would you do?

....
....
....

Day 88
Evening

Date: _____   Time: _____

What did you do today that was new?

....

....

What deserves to be celebrated or acknowledged?
How did this happen?

....

....

....

....

Where did you get off track?

....

....

....

Who will feel threatened by the changes you're
making?

....

....

....

Anything else on your mind?

....

....

....

Complete this statement. Tonight I will rest peacefully
knowing that...

....

....

Day 89
Morning

Date: _____   Time: _____

How do you feel right now?

....
....
....

What is driving this feeling?

....
....
....

How will you address the push back you are likely to receive from this forward direction?

....
....
....

How would you describe your energy level right now?

Where is this energy best directed?

....
....
....

If you knew that you would succeed at any thing you tried today, what would you do?

....
....
....

Day 89
Evening

Date: _____ Time: _____

What did you do today that was new?

....
....
....

What deserves to be celebrated or acknowledged?
How did this happen?

....
....
....
....

Where did you get off track?

....
....
....

What are you wiling to do to continue to move forward?

....
....
....

Anything else on your mind?

....
....
....

Complete this statement. Tonight I will rest peacefully knowing that...

....
....

Day 90
Morning

Date: _____   Time: _____

How do you feel right now?

....

....

....

What is driving this feeling?

....

....

....

What additional boundaries need to be put into place to support your progress.

....

....

....

How would you describe your energy level right now?

Where is this energy best directed?

....

....

If you knew that you would succeed at any thing you tried today, what would you do?

....

....

....

Day 90
Evening

Date: Time:

What did you do today that was new?

....
....
....

What deserves to be celebrated or acknowledged?
How did this happen?

....
....
....
....
....

Where did you get off track?

....
....
....

How did you expose yourself to excellence today?

....
....
....

Anything else on your mind?

....
....
....

Complete this statement. Tonight I will rest peacefully
knowing that...

....
....
....

Day 90 Review

A look back as you move forward Date: _____ Time: _____

What stands out for you?

....
....
....
....
....

What did you make progress on? How did you do it?

....
....
....
....
....

What did you not make progress on? What happened?

....
....
....
....
....

What opportunities did you see and not step into?

....
....
....
....

Reflections and Celebrations

Date: Time:

and then...

...and then

Date: .... Time: ....

What 3-5 "new things" were a pleasant surprise?

In what ways have you shifted because of this journey?

Describe how your life has changed as a result of this shift.

What new opportunities have surfaced?

How has this experience impacted the lives of those around you?

What else stands out for you?

...and then

Date: _____ Time: _____

One idea you would like to explore.

....
....
....

Where do you need support? How will you find it?

....
....
....

In what areas are you able to support someone else?
How will you gauge your capacity for this?

....
....
....

What FIERCE move forward are you going to take now?

....
....
....

This journey has been...

....
....
....
....